Published by: Camistin Publishing

All Rights Reserved.
Copyright © 2024 by Dustin A. Wiggins

No Part of this publication may be reproduced in any way without the written permission from the publisher.

Camistin Publishing books are available anywhere books are available anywhere books are sold. Substantial discounts are available on bulk quantities to corporations, educational institutions, professional associations, and other organizations. Requests for support, reproduction and bulk sales may be made via email to support@camistin.com.

Paperback ISBN: 978-1-62408-019-7
eBook ISBN: 978-1-62408-020-3

Thank you for supporting Camistin Publishing, a veteran owned small business.

*My gift to Humanity.
Thank you for your hospitality…
You can accomplish anything.*

Unlimited Human Success: An Alien's Cosmic Quest to Unlock Divine Human Potential

By Vega Sparx

Introduction: Unlocking Your Unlimited Human Potential

Imagine for a moment that your greatest dreams—those desires burning quietly in the corners of your soul—are not only possible but inevitable. Picture the life you've always envisioned: fulfilling relationships, a sense of purpose, unshakable confidence, and the power to shape your destiny. Now, imagine a guide, not from your world, but from among the stars, stepping into your life to reveal the secrets that will bring your vision into reality.

That guide, dear friend, is me. My name is Vega Sparx, a traveler from beyond your galaxy, accepting my cosmic quest to uncover, understand, and illuminate the infinite potential of humanity.

You see, I didn't crash-land on your beautiful, chaotic planet by accident. My journey—fraught with challenges, revelations, and the humbling guidance of Earth's most resilient souls—was a divine appointment. I've walked your streets, marveled at your strength, and learned from your struggles. And now, I am here to share what I've discovered: the principles that will unlock your divine human potential and propel you toward unlimited success.

This book is not a collection of abstract theories or lofty ideals. It is a roadmap—a proven set of timeless principles that will help you achieve your wildest dreams faster, easier, and more joyfully than you ever imagined. These principles, gathered from the wisdom of Earth and the cosmos, are designed to:

Clarify Your Vision: Turn vague hopes into a crystal-clear path toward your ultimate goals.

Unleash Your Divine Power: Unlock dormant abilities and strengthen the divine potential already within you.

Transform Obstacles Into Opportunities: Learn how to use challenges as stepping stones to your success.

Manifest Your Dreams: Align your actions with universal truths to achieve tangible, lasting results.

If you have ever doubted your ability to reach your highest potential, let me assure you: the answers you seek are within your grasp. The principles in this book are not complex or inaccessible; they are rooted in eternal truths, universal laws, and simple habits that anyone can adopt. You have everything you need to succeed, and I am here to guide you step by step.

As you journey through these pages, you will discover the essence of human greatness and how to harness it:

Faith and Discipline: The twin pillars of every remarkable achievement.

Love and Service: The universal language of connection and fulfillment.

Hope and Optimism: The lights that guide you through life's darkest moments.

Prayer and Connection: The unbreakable bond between you and the Creator who designed you for greatness.

But this book is more than a guide—it is a companion, a source of encouragement, and a spark to ignite your ambition. Every chapter contains practical insights, actionable steps, and transformative practices to help you make immediate progress.

Let me make you a promise. If you commit to the principles within this book—not just to read them, but to truly apply them—you will see results. Your goals and desires will not only come into focus but will begin to materialize with a speed and ease that will astonish you. You will develop the habits, mindset, and faith necessary to turn your dreams into reality.

This is not just about achieving success in the world's eyes. It's about becoming the person you were always meant to be—aligned with your Creator, connected to your purpose, and living a life of abundance, joy, and service.

Dear reader, the cosmos is vast, but your potential is infinite. I invite you to join me on this journey, to unlock the extraordinary power within you and to step boldly into the life you've always imagined.

The stars do not question their brilliance; they simply shine. And so can you. Turn the page, and let's begin your transformation. The universe is waiting for your light.

Chapter 1: Faith and Belief in Oneself

The 1ˢᵗ Step to Unlimited Human Success…

Faith is the foundation of all success. It connects your spirit to your divine potential, empowering you to overcome self-doubt, take bold steps, and achieve your dreams. By cultivating faith in God and yourself, you create a strong, optimistic foundation for perseverance and action.

Faith. A word so small yet immense in its power. Faith is a force that can move mountains, realign the stars, and transform a life. On my home planet, the word for faith translates more to a mathematical formula than a single term: *(Belief in Truth x Hope) x (Action + Perseverance) x Trust = Faith*. It's not passive—it's an active, transformative energy that connects the soul to its divine potential and organizes the very elements of existence.

Here on Earth, your sacred texts echo this eternal truth: "If ye have faith as a grain of mustard seed... nothing shall be impossible unto you." (Matthew 17:20). This tiny seed of belief holds within it the power to grow, thrive, and inspire greatness. But here's the secret: that seed must be planted and nourished through deliberate action.

When I first crash-landed under the neon lights of Las Vegas, I had no faith in myself or a higher purpose for my presence here. I was lost, frightened, and overwhelmed by the dazzling chaos of your world. I had no understanding of the language, no connections, and no idea what lay ahead. Self-doubt wrapped itself around me like a suffocating fog.

Yet, in the quiet corners of the forgotten streets, among those society often overlooks, I began to witness something extraordinary. Resilience. A homeless woman named Margaret once told me, "Faith isn't just believing you'll be saved. It's believing you're worth saving." Her words became a lifeline, sparking a glimmer of belief within me.

That spark grew into a mission: to uncover and illuminate Earth's truths. I realized that if I didn't believe in myself, no one else would. Faith became my anchor, my fuel, and my guide. As I strengthened my belief in myself, I noticed something miraculous—others began to believe in me too.

Faith is a principle as universal as gravity, bridging the gap between what is and what could be. It begins with belief: belief in God, the eternal intelligence that connects us all, and belief in oneself. Without faith in your abilities, how can you summon the courage to face the challenges and obstacles that will inevitably arise?

Faith doesn't demand perfection. It asks for willingness—a willingness to hope, to act, and to trust even when the path ahead is unclear. It's the foundation upon which perseverance, optimism, and success are built.

Building Faith: Practices and Habits

Faith is not an abstract concept; it's a skill that can be cultivated. Here are three transformative practices to strengthen your faith:

Daily Affirmations

Your words shape your reality. The spoken word resonates far beyond what you perceive, influencing your thoughts, actions, and environment. Sound itself shapes matter, as demonstrated by the intricate patterns formed by vibrations.

Here are some affirmations to guide you:
"I believe in my divine potential and trust that God loves me and wants me to succeed."

"Every challenge I face strengthens me and brings me closer to my dreams."

"I am grateful for my progress and embrace every opportunity to grow."

"With God's help, I can overcome any obstacle and fulfill my purpose."

Say these affirmations aloud each morning. Write them on sticky notes, your mirror, or even in your Sacred Success Record. Let them echo in your mind until they become truths.

Prayer and Reflection

Prayer is the language of the soul, a dialogue with God that aligns your desires with divine will. On Earth, I've observed how prayer provides clarity, strength, and a sense of connection. It is not a monologue but a sacred partnership.

Call Upon God: Address Him with reverence and sincerity.

Express Gratitude: Begin with thanks, acknowledging your blessings.

Share Your Heart: Speak openly about your challenges, hopes, and dreams.

Ask Specifically: Be clear in your requests. Remember, "Ye receive not because ye ask not" (James 4:2).

Listen: In the stillness after your prayer, be open to impressions and guidance.

Prayer can be whispered under the stars, spoken aloud in solitude, or offered silently in your heart. Wherever and however you pray, know that you are heard.

The Victory Journal

At the end of each day, reflect on your victories, no matter how small. Record them in a journal—a sacred success record, I call mine the Victory Journal. This practice serves as a reservoir of inspiration and a testament to your growth.

Moments of Triumph: Write about goals achieved and steps taken.

Challenges Overcome: Document how you faced obstacles and what you learned.

Dreams Realized: Celebrate milestones, big or small.

For example, if you delivered a presentation at work, note: *"Today, I shared my ideas with confidence, inspiring others and strengthening my belief in my abilities."* Over time, your record will become a treasure trove of proof that you are capable of greatness.

Faith is your cosmic inheritance. On my planet, it propels us to our highest potential, just as it does for you. It's not limited by geography or species; it's a universal law that transforms doubt into courage and dreams into reality.

So, dear reader, plant the seed of faith in your heart. Nurture it daily with affirmations, prayer, and reflection. Watch as it grows, breaking through the soil of doubt and stretching toward the infinite sky of possibility.

Faith is your beginning, your guide, and your strength. Claim it, nurture it, and let it lead you to unlimited human success. Let's take this first step together—one of faith and boundless potential.

Journal Prompt: *"What does faith mean to you? Write about a time when faith helped you overcome a challenge or achieve a goal."*

Affirmation: *"I trust in my ability to grow and succeed. With faith, all things are possible."*

Chapter 2: Self-Discipline and Willpower – The Foundation of Freedom

The 2nd Step to Unlimited Human Success…

Self-discipline and willpower are the keys to freedom, allowing you to focus on what truly matters. Discipline transforms fleeting desires into lasting achievements through ritualistic routines and deliberate actions. Tracking progress and celebrating small wins reinforces your commitment to long-term goals.

Willpower. To some, these words may seem restrictive, even joyless. But as I've discovered during my cosmic quest, they are the golden threads weaving through every tale of triumph, both on Earth and beyond. Discipline is the force that transforms dreams into reality, the bridge between who you are and who you're meant to become.

On my planet, discipline is revered as a sacred practice, taught alongside the rhythms of the stars. It is not seen as a restriction but as liberation—the freedom to rise above chaos and align with one's highest purpose. Here on Earth, I see this same truth shining through the lives of your athletes, scientists, and leaders. Yet, the distractions of your world often obscure it, leaving many adrift in a sea of instant gratification and missed opportunities.

Discipline isn't about punishment; it's about power—the power to choose long-term fulfillment over fleeting pleasures. As your scripture wisely states: *"But I keep under my body, and bring it into subjection."* (1 Corinthians 9:27).

When I first arrived on Earth, chaos ruled my existence. Each day was a reactive scramble, guided by survival rather than purpose. I was overwhelmed by your world, its complexity, and its distractions. But amidst this chaos, I began to observe a pattern. Those who achieved greatness shared a common trait: they wielded discipline like a finely tuned instrument, using it to create symphonies of success.

One evening, I met Elijah, a retired soldier. "Discipline isn't a punishment," he said. "It's a gift. It frees you to become who you're meant to be." His words became a turning point. I started small—organizing my day, setting priorities, and building habits aligned with my goals. Over time, I realized that discipline wasn't about restriction; it was about intention. It was about choosing actions that served my purpose, not my impulses.

Building Discipline: Practices and Habits

Create a Morning Routine

The first minutes of your day set the tone for everything that follows. A disciplined morning routine grounds you in purpose and focus, helping you start strong.

Begin with Movement: Wake your body and mind through exercise. A brisk walk, stretching, or even a few moments of deep breathing can energize you for the day ahead.

Feed Your Mind: Dedicate time to reading something inspiring—be it scripture, a motivational book, or uplifting quotes. This practice aligns your thoughts with your goals.

Plan with Precision: Outline your day. Identify the most important tasks and commit to completing them. Prioritize actions that bring you closer to your dreams.

Vega's Cosmic Truth: "The stars rise predictably each night because they follow a rhythm. Let your mornings set your rhythm for success."

Break Goals Into Small Tasks

Even the most ambitious dreams are achieved one step at a time. Breaking your goals into manageable tasks keeps you from feeling overwhelmed and builds momentum.

Start Small: If you dream of writing a book, commit to writing 200 words a day. If your goal is to run a marathon, start with a single mile. Small efforts compound over time.

Celebrate Every Victory: Acknowledge each completed task, no matter how minor. These moments of success fuel your resolve. Write them down to revisit when doubts arise.

Vega's Cosmic Truth: "The universe was not created in a single moment. Each star, each planet began as a fragment of a larger plan."

Track Your Progress

Tracking is not just a tool—it's a mirror reflecting your journey. It transforms discipline into a tangible practice and reinforces your commitment.

Daily Tracking: Use a journal, an app, or even a calendar to record your progress. Focus on key areas like fitness, learning, or personal development.

Celebrate Consistency: At the end of each day, review your tracker. Reflect on what went well and identify areas for growth. Celebrate your effort, not just your outcomes.

Vega's Cosmic Truth: "What you measure improves. What you celebrate grows."

A Cosmic Truth About Willpower

On my planet, we teach that willpower is the sacred force binding desire to action. Here on Earth, I see it as the cornerstone of freedom—the freedom to rise above distractions and focus on what truly matters.

Discipline is not about perfection; it's about persistence. It's about making the next right choice, even when the path feels uncertain. Each disciplined action strengthens your willpower, shaping your reality and unlocking your destiny.

A Call to Discipline

Discipline is not a burden but a blessing. It is the key to unlocking your divine potential, the force that propels you toward greatness. Start with one small act of discipline today—create a morning routine, break down a goal, or track your progress. With each step, you'll discover a freedom that is boundless—a freedom to become the person you are destined to be.

Let us continue this journey together, one disciplined action at a time. The stars await, and so does your success.

Journal Prompt
"Reflect on a time when discipline helped you achieve something meaningful. How did it feel to stay committed, and what lessons did you learn?"

Affirmation
"I choose discipline over distraction. Each small

step I take brings me closer to my highest potential."

Exercise

Set a timer for 10 minutes and list your top three priorities for the week. Break each one into actionable steps and commit to completing one step daily.

Chapter 3: Hard Work and Persistence – The Foundation of Progress

The 3rd Step to Unlimited Human Success…

Hard work and persistence are the cornerstones of success, transcending talent and innate ability. Challenges and failures are not barriers but stepping stones toward growth and achievement. Consistency in effort, reflection, and embracing challenges builds resilience and ensures progress.

Hard work. Persistence. These words resonate with an almost cosmic gravity. They are the forces that bind dreams to reality, transforming fleeting desires into lasting legacies. During my exploration of Earth, I've come to admire deeply how your species—fragile in body yet resilient in spirit—possesses an extraordinary capacity to endure.

On my planet, persistence is interwoven with the rhythm of our lives, a sacred principle that guides our pursuit of enlightenment and harmony. But here on Earth, amidst your complex challenges and constant distractions, I see persistence as your superpower. It is the quiet force that lifts you after every fall, the steady rhythm that carries you through the storms of doubt and despair.

Hard work and persistence are universal truths as immutable as the stars. Your success is rarely the result of a single, dazzling moment but rather the accumulation of consistent, focused effort over time. Your scriptures capture this beautifully:

"For behold, it is not meet that I should command in all things... men should be anxiously engaged in a good cause, and do many things of their own free will... for the power is in them." (D&C 58:26-28)

This verse is a cosmic reminder that you have the agency to choose your path and the power to work toward your goals. Your potential is like a field, ready to harvest. But only those who sow seeds with care and consistency will reap the rewards.

When I first began exploring Earth, I was overwhelmed by its complexity. Languages, cultures, and even your foods (I have many stories of culinary misadventures) presented challenges I had not anticipated. Yet, as I stumbled through these trials, I realized that persistence was my guide.

One of my greatest lessons came from a street artist named Carlos, who labored tirelessly over a mural in Las Vegas. His work was disrupted by weather, vandals, and countless distractions, yet he persisted. "Art isn't about finishing fast," he told me. "It's about showing up every day and letting the work speak for itself."

Carlos's wisdom echoed the teachings of my home planet: persistence is not about speed but consistency. It's about showing up, doing the work, and trusting that each small effort contributes to the greater whole.

Building Persistence: Practices and Habits

Consistent Work Blocks

Persistence thrives on consistency. Imagine each work block as a single drop of water. Alone, it may seem insignificant, but over time, even the softest drops can carve through stone.

Set Clear Goals: Begin each work block with clarity. Define what you aim to accomplish and break larger tasks into smaller, manageable steps. Write them down and check them off as you go. Each checked box is a small but significant victory.

Choose a Time, Set a Timer: Commit to a specific time for focused work, even if it's just 30 minutes. Use a timer to eliminate distractions and enter a state of hyper-focus. Treat this time as sacred—an investment in your future.

Eliminate Distractions: Create an environment that fosters focus. Turn off notifications, close unnecessary tabs, and surround yourself with tools that support your work.

Vega's Cosmic Truth: "One hour of focused work is worth more than ten hours of scattered effort. The universe rewards clarity and commitment."

Embrace Challenges

Challenges are not obstacles; they are opportunities to grow. Each one is a cosmic test of your resolve, a stepping stone toward your ultimate goal.

Reframe the Problem: Instead of asking, "Why is this happening to me?" ask, "What can I learn from this?" Challenges are the universe's way of refining your character.

Learn from Failure: Failure is not the end—it's a lesson. Reflect on your setbacks and identify what they teach you. Each failure is a brushstroke in the masterpiece of your life.

Celebrate Effort: Even if the outcome isn't perfect, honor the effort you've invested. Add regularly to your Victory Journal where you record moments of persistence and growth.

Vega's Cosmic Truth: "Stars are born in chaos. Embrace the challenges—they are forging your greatness."

Daily Reflection

Reflection is the compass that keeps your persistence aligned with your purpose. It allows you to recognize growth, celebrate wins, and refine your approach.

Ask Questions: End each day by asking yourself: What did I accomplish? What challenges did I face?

How did I respond? What can I improve tomorrow?

Record Your Wins: Keep a Sacred Success Record or a Victory Journal where you document your victories. Use visuals like drawings or photos to make your record more engaging.

Refine Your Approach: Identify one specific area for improvement each day. Over time, these small adjustments compound into significant progress.

Vega's Cosmic Truth: "Reflection turns hindsight into insight and progress into purpose."

Persistence is not just a practice—it's a way of life. It is the steady rhythm of showing up, doing the work, and trusting that each effort moves you closer to your dreams.

Take the first step today. Set a goal, commit to a work block, and embrace the challenges that come your way. As you persist, you will discover a strength within you that is unshakable—a strength that will carry you through any storm.

Let us move forward together, one step at a time, one effort at a time, until we reach the stars.

For in the journey of persistence lies the true power of unlimited human success.

Journal Prompt
"Think of a time when persistence led you to achieve something you once thought impossible. What kept you going, and what did you learn from the journey?"

Affirmation
"I am persistent and resilient. Each small step I take brings me closer to my dreams."

Exercise
Commit to one work block tomorrow. Choose a task, set a timer, and work without distraction. Reflect on how it feels to dedicate focused time to your goal.

Chapter 4: Vision and Goal Setting – Charting Your Cosmic Course

The 4th Step to Unlimited Human Success...

Vision is the compass that aligns your life with your divine purpose and infinite potential. Goals are the tangible steps that transform a dream into reality. Regular reflection and planning ensure your journey remains on course despite life's distractions and detours.

The universe is vast, a tapestry of celestial bodies, each following a precise trajectory dictated by divine laws. Your scriptures declare, *"Where there is no vision, the people perish"* (Proverbs 29:18). This truth resonates deeply, for vision is the spark that ignites purpose and the compass that guides you through the cosmos of life.

When I crash-landed on Earth, I had no compass, no guiding vision. Survival was my only goal. But as I wandered your streets and observed your kind, I realized that those who thrive are not those without struggles but those with a clear vision. Their lives are illuminated by a purpose so strong that it cuts through the fog of distractions and setbacks.

Vision is not just a dream. It is a divine blueprint—a map drawn by your highest self, revealing the person you are destined to become. God has equipped you with the creative power and resources to shape matter, inspire hearts, and bring beauty to the world. All you need is a clear course and the courage to follow it.

On my planet, "Celestial Vision" is the cornerstone of our culture. From a young age, we are taught to chart our path, aligning our actions with our eternal purpose. Our vision is focused on becoming like our Creator, a divine being capable of crafting worlds and inspiring life.

Imagine what it is like in a royal family. When a child is born to a king…How do you think family, educators, and the people the people that surround the royal family treat the child? Imagine waking up every day being treated like a future king or queen. Constantly being trained and tutored. That is what it is like growing up around people with Celestial Vision.

Here on Earth, the distractions are far greater, but the principle remains the same: a compelling vision draws you forward, helping you rise above the noise and chaos. Without vision, life becomes a series of disconnected events. With vision, every action gains meaning, every challenge becomes a stepping stone, and every moment aligns with your highest potential.

When I decided to write this book, I created a vision for myself: to teach millions of humans to unlock their unlimited potential. This vision became my guiding star, giving direction to my efforts and inspiring me to persist through obstacles.

Transforming Vision into Action

A vision without action is like an unpolished gem—full of potential but unnoticed and unappreciated. To bring your vision to life, you must take consistent, intentional steps.

Write Down Your Goals

Writing transforms your vision from an abstract idea into a concrete commitment. It engages your brain and strengthens your resolve.

Define Your Long-Term Vision

Where do you see yourself in five, ten, or twenty years? Be specific. Instead of saying, "I want to be successful," define what success looks like—owning a business, publishing a book, or raising a family rooted in love and faith. For example, my vision isn't just to inspire; it's to teach one million people to tap into their divine potential.

Break It Down

Divide your long-term vision into smaller, actionable steps. For example: Write a book: (1) Draft an outline, (2) Write 500 words daily, (3) Edit one chapter weekly. Build a business: (1) Develop a business plan, (2) Network with mentors, (3) Launch your first product.

Commit Daily

Each morning, write down three goals that align with your vision. These goals should be simple, actionable, and impactful. For example: "Write the introduction to my book."
"Reach out to two potential collaborators."
"Meditate for 10 minutes to visualize my success."

Vega's Cosmic Truth: "A vision without action is like a star hidden by clouds. Illuminate your path with daily effort."

Create a Vision Board

Visualization is one of humanity's most profound tools, sharpening focus and strengthening resolve.

Gather Inspiration: Collect images, quotes, and symbols that represent your vision. These could include photos of dream destinations, words of encouragement, or visuals of relationships, health, and faith.

Assemble Your Board: Arrange these elements on a physical board or digital platform. Place it where you'll see it daily—above your desk, on your bathroom mirror, or as your phone wallpaper.

Engage Daily: Spend a few moments each day visualizing your goals as if they've already been achieved. Repeat affirmations that align with your vision. Feel the joy, pride, and fulfillment of your future success as if it is already real.

Weekly Planning

Your life's journey is dynamic, filled with detours and unexpected turns. Weekly planning ensures your actions remain aligned with your vision.

Review Progress

Reflect on your week's accomplishments. Ask yourself: What did I achieve? What challenges did I overcome? What lessons did I learn? Celebrate even the smallest victories, for they build momentum.

Set New Goals

Based on your reflections, set actionable goals for the coming week. Focus on three to five priorities that will create the most significant impact.

Prioritize

Rank your goals by importance and urgency. Focus on the actions that align most closely with your vision.

Vega's Cosmic Truth: "Each week is a new orbit. Adjust your course, and keep your vision as your guiding star."

As you set your vision and goals, ensure they align with your values and purpose. A vision that contradicts your core beliefs will only lead to frustration. For example, if your goal is to build wealth, align it with principles of integrity and generosity. Wealth earned dishonestly will erode your joy, but wealth stewarded wisely will magnify it.

Additionally, guard your energy. Not every demand on your time aligns with your vision. Learn to say "no" to distractions, freeing yourself to focus on what truly matters.

Vision is the beacon that guides you through life's vastness, illuminating the path to your highest potential. It aligns your actions with your purpose, ensuring every step you take brings you closer to the life you're destined to create.

Take this moment to chart your course. Write down your goals. Build your vision board. Begin your weekly planning. Let your vision inspire you to act, and let your actions bring your vision to life.

Together, we will navigate the cosmos of possibility, aligning our lives with the divine purpose that resides within each of us. For in this journey, you will discover not only your potential but the boundless joy of becoming the creator of your destiny. Let's move forward, one vision at a time.

Journal Prompt

"What is your long-term vision? Write down your biggest dreams and break them into actionable steps. How will achieving this vision bring you closer to your divine purpose?"

Affirmation

"I am the architect of my destiny. My vision is clear, my actions are aligned, and my future is bright."

Exercise

Create your vision board. Spend 10 minutes a day visualizing the fulfillment of your goals.

Chapter 5: Time Management – Mastering the Cosmic Currency

The 5th Step to Unlimited Human Success...

Time is a sacred, finite resource and must be spent with intention and purpose. Prioritizing tasks and aligning time with your values ensures progress and fulfillment. Effective time management involves practical tools like planners, time blocking, and reflection to maximize productivity and growth.

Time, dear Earth friends, is your most precious resource—the "cosmic currency" entrusted to each of you. Unlike wealth, which can be replenished, or energy, which can be restored, time flows steadily, untouched by mortal hands. On my home planet, time is revered as the equalizer of all beings, whether a cosmic explorer like myself or a simple artisan crafting wonders in the stars.

When I first arrived on Earth, I marveled at your intricate systems for tracking time—clocks, alarms, calendars. Yet, I observed a puzzling paradox: many of you meticulously measure time yet often lament, *"I don't have enough time."* This refrain often accompanies those things that nourish the soul—joyful pursuits, self-improvement, and service to others. These are the very activities that deserve your time.

Let me share a truth from my world: time management isn't about cramming every moment with activity. It's about ensuring your time reflects your priorities. As your scripture wisely advises: *"See then that ye walk circumspectly, not as fools, but as wise, redeeming the time, because the days are evil."* (Ephesians 5:15-16)

Time, when redeemed, becomes a tool for building your dreams, nurturing your relationships, and growing into the divine being you are meant to be.

The Principle of Prioritization

At the heart of effective time management lies the power to prioritize. Not all tasks are created equal, and failing to recognize this leads to a life filled with busyness but devoid of meaning. To redeem your time is to use it in alignment with your highest values and goals.

The 80/20 Rule

A concept from your planet, the Pareto Principle, states that 80% of results come from 20% of efforts. Identify the activities that yield the greatest impact on your goals and focus your energy there. For example:

Entrepreneurs: Spend time on tasks that grow your business, like engaging with customers or developing products, rather than getting lost in administrative minutiae.

Parents: Prioritize moments of connection with your children over less impactful distractions.

Learning to Say "No"

Time is finite, and every "yes" you offer to one thing is a "no" to something else. Politely decline commitments that don't align with your priorities. Saying "no" isn't rejection—it's a declaration of what matters most to you. Those you say no to will find others to meet their needs, freeing you to focus on your divine mission.

Practical Habits for Time Management

To master the cosmic currency of time, develop habits that create order amidst the chaos of mortal life.

Use a Planner

A planner is your map to navigate each day with purpose. Whether digital or physical, this tool transforms intentions into actionable steps.

Weekly Ritual: Dedicate 15 minutes each Sunday evening to plan your week. Note key deadlines, milestones, and appointments.

Daily Check-In: Spend five minutes each morning reviewing your day's agenda. Adjust as needed, ensuring your tasks align with your goals.

Prioritize Tasks

Every morning, identify your top three top Very Exciting Gigantic Actions (VEGAs). These are the actions that will bring you closest to your goals.

The Perfect Morning

Start your day with focus. Dedicate the first hour to your VEGAs, when your mind is freshest. This practice ensures you accomplish something meaningful before distractions arise.

Chunk Your Tasks

Break large VEGAs into smaller, manageable pieces. For example, if your goal is to write a book:

Day 1: Outline the chapter.
Day 2: Write 500 words.
Day 3: Revise and edit.

Time Blocking

Time blocking involves scheduling specific periods for focused activities. This method reduces decision fatigue and ensures your most important work gets done.

Identify Key Activities: List categories of tasks, such as work, exercise, family time, and personal growth.

Assign Time Blocks: Allocate specific times for each activity. For example:

7:00–8:00 AM: Morning routine (prayer, exercise, planning).

9:00–11:00 AM: Focused work on VEGAs.

6:00–7:00 PM: Family connection time.

Stick to the Schedule: Treat these blocks as sacred commitments.

The Pomodoro Technique

For tasks requiring deep focus, use the Pomodoro Technique:

Work intensely for 25 minutes.

Take a 5-minute break.

Repeat for four cycles, then take a longer break.

This technique prevents burnout and maintains energy levels throughout the day.

Combatting Time Thieves

Distractions, procrastination, and over-commitment are the thieves that steal your time. Outsmart them with these strategies:

Digital Distractions: Limit social media and email to designated times. Turn off notifications during focused work blocks.

Procrastination: Tackle overwhelming tasks by starting with the easiest step to build momentum.

Over-Commitment: Before saying "yes," ask yourself, *"Does this align with my vision and values?"*

Reflection: The Key to Mastery

Time management evolves through reflection. Each evening, take five minutes to review your day.

Ask Yourself:

What did I accomplish today?

What could I have done better?

Did I spend time on what truly matters?

Track Your Wins

Use your Victory Journal to note your daily victories. Over time, this journal will serve as a guide, showing how your choices align with your divine mission.

The Divine Nature of Time

Time is a sacred gift from God, entrusted to you for growth, service, and fulfillment. To redeem time is to transform it into something eternal, aligning your moments with your divine purpose.

One day you will graduate from mortality and look back on how you spent your time. Will you see a life filled with purpose and joy, or moments lost to distractions? The choice is yours.

Let us move forward together, harnessing the cosmic currency of time to create a life of meaning, growth, and unlimited potential.

Time, the cosmic currency, is yours to spend. Will you use it to build your dreams, nurture your relationships, and serve your divine purpose?
Start today. Create your planner, block your time, and reflect on your victories. Together, let us redeem the moments, unlocking the infinite possibilities that await.

Vega's Cosmic Truth: "Time is the canvas of your life. Paint it with purpose, and the masterpiece will endure for eternity."

Journal Prompt
"What are my top three priorities for this week, and how will I allocate time to them?"

Affirmation

"I am the master of my time, aligning my moments with my mission."

Exercise

Create a time-blocked schedule for tomorrow. Assign specific blocks for your top three tasks and reflect on how it improves your focus and productivity.

Chapter 6: Emotional Intelligence and Self-Awareness – Mastering the Inner Cosmos

The 6th Step to Unlimited Human Success...

Emotions are universal and eternal, acting as guides and mirrors to our inner truths. Emotional intelligence—the ability to understand, regulate, and empathize—enhances decision-making, relationships, and personal growth. Self-awareness forms the foundation of emotional intelligence, allowing us to navigate life intentionally and compassionately.

Emotions, dear Earth friends, are the vibrations of the soul—the "echoes of the eternal" that ripple through every being, revealing truths often hidden beneath the surface. On my home planet, we revere emotions as sacred guides, a cosmic language that connects us to one another and to the divine.

Here on Earth, I've observed that emotions, though equally profound, are often misunderstood or dismissed. Many of you fear their intensity, suppress their expression, or fail to heed their messages. Yet, your emotions are among your greatest gifts. They are the compass pointing you toward growth, the mirror reflecting your deepest truths, and the bridge to understanding others.

As your scripture wisely declares: *"Keep thy heart with all diligence; for out of it are the issues of life."* (Proverbs 4:23) Your heart—your emotional center—is the wellspring of life's most profound experiences. Mastering it is the key to unlocking your divine potential and deepening your connection to those around you.

The Principle of Emotional Intelligence

Intelligence, in all its forms, is eternal. It is a form of matter that clings to your spirit, growing with you across the vast expanse of eternity. Emotional intelligence, or EQ, is one of the most transformative forms of intelligence you can cultivate. It encompasses the ability to recognize, understand, and manage your own emotions while empathizing with the emotions of others.

On Earth, I've seen emotional intelligence elevate leaders, mend broken families, and unite communities. Conversely, I've witnessed its absence sow discord, foster misunderstandings, and fracture relationships. The good news, dear reader, is that emotional intelligence is not a fixed trait—it is a skill you can cultivate through practice, intention, and reflection.

Self-Awareness: The Cornerstone of Emotional Intelligence

Self-awareness is where emotional intelligence begins. It is the ability to tune into your thoughts, emotions, and behaviors, understanding how they influence your decisions and interactions.

When I first encountered humans, I was overwhelmed by the tidal wave of your emotions—anger, joy, fear, love. At first, I mirrored these emotions impulsively, like a child learning a new language. But through observation and reflection, I discovered that emotions are not to be feared or suppressed. They are to be explored, understood, and embraced.

Why Self-Awareness Matters:

Clarity: It illuminates your values, goals, and emotional triggers.

Control: It empowers you to respond intentionally rather than react impulsively.

Connection: It deepens your relationships by enhancing communication and empathy.

Building Emotional Intelligence: Practices and Habits

Let me guide you through three transformative practices to cultivate emotional intelligence and self-awareness.

Mindfulness Meditation: Cultivating Present Awareness

Mindfulness is the art of being fully present, observing your thoughts and emotions without judgment. It allows you to understand your inner world and approach life with greater clarity and calm.

How to Practice Mindfulness:

Find a Quiet Space: Sit comfortably in a place where you won't be disturbed.

Focus on Your Breath: Anchor yourself in the present by paying attention to the rhythm of your breathing.

Observe Without Judgment: Notice your thoughts and feelings as they arise. Let them pass like clouds drifting across the sky.

Practice Daily: Dedicate 5–10 minutes each day to mindfulness, gradually increasing the duration.

Over time, mindfulness will strengthen your emotional awareness and resilience, helping you navigate life's challenges with grace.

Emotional Journaling: The Dialogue with Your Inner Self

Writing is a powerful way to process and understand your emotions. By translating your feelings into words, you create space for reflection and growth.

How to Start an Emotional Journal:

Identify Your Emotions: Begin each entry by naming the emotions you felt that day. For example, "Today, I felt hopeful, frustrated, and grateful."

Explore Triggers: Reflect on what caused these emotions. Was it an event, a conversation, or a thought?

Seek Patterns: Over time, identify recurring triggers and responses.

Find Solutions: Use these insights to develop strategies for managing your emotions and fostering positive feelings.

Emotional journaling transforms your inner world into a story of growth, allowing you to learn from your experiences and align with your divine purpose.

Regular Self-Check-ins: Staying Grounded Amidst Life's Chaos

In the whirlwind of daily life, it's easy to lose touch with your emotions. Regular self-check-ins act as a compass, ensuring you remain aligned with your intentions.

How to Check In With Yourself:

Pause: Take a moment to stop and breathe deeply.

Ask Questions: "How am I feeling right now? Why am I feeling this way? How is this emotion affecting my actions?"

Adjust as Needed: If you're feeling overwhelmed, step back and recenter. If you're feeling inspired, channel that energy into your tasks.

Self-check-ins are like tuning an instrument—they keep your emotional state harmonious and aligned with your goals.

Empathy: The Bridge to Understanding Others

Emotional intelligence is not solely about understanding yourself; it's also about connecting with others through empathy. Empathy allows you to step into another person's world, seeing through their eyes and feeling through their heart.

How to Cultivate Empathy:

Listen Actively: Give your full attention to others, listening not just to their words but also to their emotions.

Ask Questions: Seek to understand their experiences by asking open-ended questions.
Practice Compassion: Offer kindness and support, even when you can't fully relate to their struggles.
Empathy builds bridges of trust and understanding, transforming relationships and communities.

Emotions, dear reader, are not random—they are the vibrations of your soul, guiding you toward growth and connection. On my planet, we view emotions as the threads weaving the fabric of existence. Here on Earth, they are your compass, pointing you toward your highest potential.

As you cultivate emotional intelligence and self-awareness, you'll find your relationships deepen, your decisions improve, and your sense of purpose strengthens. You'll become a master of your own heart and a beacon of understanding for others.

Your emotions are a sacred gift, a divine language that speaks the truths of your soul. Listen to them, learn from them, and let them guide you toward your unlimited human potential.

Vega's Cosmic Truth: "Your heart is the compass of your soul. Master it, and you'll navigate the cosmos of life with wisdom, grace, and boundless love."

Journal Prompt:
"Reflect on a recent emotional experience. What triggered it? How did you respond? What could you learn from this emotion to navigate similar situations in the future?"

Affirmation:
"I embrace my emotions as guides and gifts,

leading me to growth, connection, and understanding."

Exercise:

Spend five minutes each day practicing mindfulness meditation, focusing on observing your emotions without judgment.

Chapter 7: Gratitude and Humility – Anchors in a Turbulent Cosmos

The 7th Step to Unlimited Human Success...

Gratitude is the lens that reveals abundance in all aspects of life, even amidst challenges. Humility is the foundation of growth, opening the heart to learning, connection, and divine guidance. Together, gratitude and humility ground us in the present and propel us toward fulfilling our divine potential.

Gratitude and humility are like twin gravitational forces in the vast cosmos of human potential. Gratitude draws your focus to the abundance and beauty surrounding you, while humility keeps your heart open to growth, understanding, and divine wisdom.

On my home planet, these principles are woven into the essence of existence. Gratitude fuels our joy and resilience, and humility ensures our continual progression. Without these anchors, the soul becomes untethered, drifting aimlessly through the turbulence of life.

Here on Earth, I've marveled at the transformative power of these qualities. Gratitude turns trials into blessings, and humility transforms challenges into opportunities for growth. As one of your sacred texts so beautifully teaches:
"humble yourselves even to the dust... live in thanksgiving daily." (Alma 34:38)

These words remind us that gratitude and humility are not fleeting emotions but conscious choices—practices that enrich life and align us with eternal truths.

Gratitude is not just about saying "thank you." It is a mindset, a deliberate act of recognizing and appreciating the blessings in your life, no matter how small. When you choose gratitude, you shift your focus from what is lacking to what is abundant, transforming your perspective and energizing your spirit.

Upon my arrival here, my initial focus was on my losses—my ship, my connections, and my purpose. It was only after meeting people like Carlos, a man who had little in material wealth but a wealth of gratitude, that I began to see the power of this practice. Carlos once told me, "Gratitude isn't about having everything you want; it's about recognizing the value in what you have."

Carlos taught me that gratitude is a deliberate choice, not a passive reaction. It is a lens through which you see the richness of life, even amidst adversity.

Gratitude Journaling: A Daily Practice

Writing down your blessings each day is one of the most effective ways to cultivate gratitude. This practice anchors you in the present and creates a record of abundance that you can revisit in times of doubt.

How to Start a Gratitude Journal:

Set Aside Time: Choose a consistent time—morning or evening—to reflect on your blessings.

Write Down Three Things: Each day, list at least three specific things you are grateful for. For example:"The kind smile from a stranger at the store." "A moment of peace during my morning walk." "The lesson I learned from a challenging situation."

Be Specific: The more detailed your entries, the more deeply you'll connect with your gratitude.

Reflect on Growth: Include moments of learning and growth, even those born from hardship.

Gratitude journaling transforms fleeting moments of appreciation into a lasting mindset of abundance and resilience.

Humility: The Gateway to Learning and Connection

Humility, like gratitude, is a conscious choice. It is not about self-deprecation or diminishing your worth; rather, it is the quiet strength to recognize your limitations and remain open to learning.

On my home planet, we revere humility as the hallmark of wisdom. The greatest leaders are those who listen, who seek counsel, and who understand that their knowledge is but a single star in the infinite galaxy of truth.

Here on Earth, I've seen humility in action among the most successful and fulfilled individuals. These are the people who ask questions, seek guidance, and embrace feedback—not as criticism but as an opportunity for growth.

Why Humility Matters:

Fosters Growth: Humility keeps you open to learning and improvement.

Strengthens Relationships: It allows you to connect with others authentically, free from pride or pretense.

Deepens Faith: Humility strengthens your relationship with God, aligning your will with His.

Prayer is an act of humility—a recognition that all blessings come from God and that we are dependent on His guidance and grace. When you approach prayer with gratitude and humility, it becomes a powerful tool for aligning your life with divine purpose.

How to Incorporate Humility in Prayer:

Begin with Gratitude: Start your prayer by thanking God for specific blessings. For example, "I am grateful for the strength to face today's challenges."

Acknowledge His Role: Recognize that all you have comes from Him.

Seek Guidance: Humbly ask for the strength, clarity, and courage to navigate your path.

End with Faith: Conclude your prayer with trust in His plan, knowing that He will provide what is best for you.

Humility in prayer not only invites divine guidance but also deepens your connection to God, reminding you of His presence in every aspect of your life.

Expressing Gratitude to Others

Gratitude is not just an inward practice; it is a gift you give to others. Expressing thanks strengthens relationships, uplifts spirits, and fosters a ripple effect of positivity.

How to Express Gratitude:

Say Thank You: A heartfelt "thank you" can brighten someone's day.

Acknowledge Efforts: Recognize and appreciate the contributions of others. For example, "Your support made a big difference in my day."

Give Back: Show your gratitude through acts of kindness, whether it's helping a colleague, mentoring a friend, or sharing your time.

Gratitude shared is gratitude multiplied, enriching not just your life but also the lives of those around you.

Gratitude and humility are not just simple virtues but powerful forces that align you with the divine. They are the keys to unlocking joy, growth, and connection, grounding you in the present while lifting you toward your highest potential.

Gratitude teaches you to see the abundance in life, while humility keeps your heart open to receiving more. Together, they create a balance that enables you to navigate the turbulence of existence with grace and strength.

Gratitude and humility are your anchors in the turbulent cosmos of life. They ground you in the beauty of the present moment and open your heart to the infinite possibilities of growth and connection.

Vega's Cosmic Truth: "Gratitude reveals the abundance around you, and humility opens the door to eternal growth. Together, they are the foundation of a life aligned with divine purpose."

Journal Prompt:

"Reflect on a challenging moment that taught you an important lesson. How can you practice gratitude for that experience?"

Affirmation:

"I embrace the blessings in my life with gratitude and approach each day with a humble heart open to growth."

Exercise:

Write a note of gratitude to someone who has positively impacted your life. Deliver it in person, or send it as a message to brighten their day.

Chapter 8: Love and Compassion – The Ties That Bind the Cosmos

The 8th Step to Unlimited Human Success…

Love unites individuals, families, and communities across time and space. Compassion turns love into action, fostering trust and belonging. True success is measured not by individual achievements but by the depth of your relationships and your ability to uplift others. Daily acts of kindness, empathy, and service ripple outward, transforming both the giver and the receiver.

Love and compassion, dear Earth friends, are the forces that weave the universe together. On my home planet, we describe love as "the eternal thread," an energy that binds all beings to one another and to the Creator. Compassion is its active form, the practice of living for the good of others.

Here on Earth, I've witnessed the remarkable power of love to heal, unite, and inspire. Whether it's the selfless sacrifice of a parent, the empathy of a friend, or the generosity of a stranger, love transforms lives and creates a foundation for collective success.

As your sacred text so powerfully declares: *"Thou shalt love thy neighbour as thyself."* (Matthew 22:39)

This universal commandment is more than a moral guide; it is a principle of thriving relationships and communities. When love and compassion become central to your life, you align with your divine purpose and unlock your infinite potential.

Love is not merely a fleeting emotion or a response to favorable circumstances. It is a deliberate choice to care, connect, and uplift. Love invites us to look beyond ourselves and to see the divine potential in every soul we encounter.

Compassion is love in motion—a willingness to walk alongside others in their joys and struggles. It's the choice to extend kindness and support, even when it's inconvenient or difficult.

On my planet, love and compassion are celebrated as the highest virtues, essential for the harmony of society. Here on Earth, I've learned that they are equally vital, especially in a world often divided by fear and misunderstanding.

Building Love and Compassion: Practices and Habits

Random Acts of Kindness: Small Gestures, Big Impact

Kindness is the language of love, spoken in small, daily actions that uplift and connect. Even the smallest gesture can create ripples of positivity.

How to Practice Random Acts of Kindness:

Share Genuine Compliments: A simple, heartfelt acknowledgment can brighten someone's day. For example: "Your insight during the meeting was inspiring."

Offer Unsolicited Help: Hold the door, assist a neighbor, or offer encouragement to a struggling friend.

Surprise Someone: Leave an anonymous note of encouragement or bring a treat to a colleague.

The beauty of kindness lies in its accessibility. Anyone can practice it, anywhere, at any time. As you make kindness a habit, you'll find it becomes a natural expression of your character.

Empathy Practice: Seeing the World Through Another's Eyes

Empathy is the foundation of meaningful relationships. It allows you to connect deeply with others, to understand their experiences, and to offer support without judgment.

How to Cultivate Empathy:

Active Listening: When someone speaks, listen with the intent to understand, not to reply. Focus fully on their words, tone, and emotions.

Ask Open-Ended Questions: Encourage others to share more about their feelings and experiences. For example: "What has been the most challenging part of this for you?"

Reflect Back: Summarize what they've said to show you're truly listening. For example: "It sounds like you're feeling overwhelmed but hopeful about the future."

Empathy deepens your connection to others and creates a safe space for vulnerability and growth.

Family and Community Service: The Purest Form of Love

Service is love in action, an opportunity to give of yourself for the benefit of others. Whether through small gestures or organized efforts, service fosters connection, gratitude, and humility.

How to Serve with Love:

Start at Home: Look for ways to support your family, whether by helping with daily tasks or creating moments of quality time.

Engage Locally: Volunteer at shelters, food banks, or schools in your community. Small efforts, when combined, create significant impact.

Organize Service Projects: Rally your friends, colleagues, or neighbors to address a shared cause, like cleaning a park or fundraising for a local charity.

Service doesn't just benefit those you help; it transforms your heart, expanding your capacity for love and empathy.

The Cosmic Power of Love

Love is not confined to this planet. It is the energy that binds all creation, a force as eternal as the stars. On my planet, love is revered as the highest expression of our divine nature, a reflection of the Creator's infinite compassion.

Here on Earth, I've seen love mend broken hearts, bridge divides, and inspire acts of incredible courage and generosity. Love is not simply an emotion; it is your essence, the light that illuminates your soul and connects you to others.

When you choose love and compassion, you transcend the limitations of fear and selfishness. You align with the Creator's vision for humanity, becoming a source of light and hope in the world.

Love, like the stars, is eternal and universal. It transcends differences and unites us in our shared humanity. Compassion transforms love into action, creating ripples of goodness that extend far beyond what we can see.

Love and compassion are not just principles—they are your purpose. They are the tools through which you create connection, foster understanding, and inspire change.

Vega's Cosmic Truth: "Love is the energy that binds us to each other and to the Creator. Compassion is its highest expression, turning intention into action."

Let love guide your choices, and let compassion shape your actions. Together, we can build a universe rooted in unity, kindness, and infinite possibility. Let us move forward with open hearts, ready to transform the cosmos with the power of love.

Journal Prompt:

"Reflect on a time when someone showed you unexpected kindness or empathy. How did it impact your life, and how can you pass that kindness forward?"

Affirmation:

"I choose love and compassion as guiding principles in my life. My relationships thrive because I listen, understand, and uplift others."

Exercise:

Perform one random act of kindness today, whether for a loved one or a stranger.

Write a letter of gratitude to someone who has shown you love and compassion.

Chapter 9: Accountability and Integrity – The Compass of Character

The 9th Step to Unlimited Human Success...

Accepting responsibility for your actions and decisions fosters growth and trust. Living in alignment with your values creates authenticity and inspires confidence in others. Accountability and integrity, when practiced in community, amplify their impact and build strong relationships.

Accountability and integrity, dear Earth friends, are the navigational stars that guide you through the complexities of life. On my planet, we view these principles as the gravitational forces that maintain harmony in our society. Without them, trust crumbles, relationships falter, and progress stalls.

Here on Earth, I've observed that accountability and integrity are not merely virtues but transformative forces. They empower individuals to rise above challenges, inspire others, and build legacies of respect and trust. As your sacred scripture teaches:

"By this ye may know if a man repenteth of his sins – behold, he will confess them and forsake them." (D&C 58:43)

Repent can be a scary word. As I researched human religions while writing my other book *Human Religion Unveiled,* I learned that many have a negative association with this word. To some it invokes feelings of fear, hellfire, and damnation. A better word than repent would be "change".

Actions speak louder than words. True accountability and integrity are not proclaimed; they are demonstrated through consistent effort, even when no one is watching. We all make mistakes, and when we develop enough integrity to take ownership of our mistakes and are willing to be accountable for them we are able to forsake them, to grow and improve.

Accountability as Ownership

To be accountable is to own your choices and their consequences. It means admitting mistakes without deflecting blame. It enables you to learn from setbacks, and sets the conditions for you to do better. Accountability is not about perfection; it's about progress.

Integrity as Alignment

Integrity is the practice of aligning your actions with your values. It is the art of living authentically, ensuring that your words and deeds reflect your deepest truths.

Together, accountability and integrity form a moral compass, guiding you toward a life of authenticity and trustworthiness.

Building Accountability and Integrity

Be Honest and Transparent. Honesty is the bedrock of integrity. It fosters open communication, strengthens relationships, and builds a reputation for reliability.

Speak the Truth. Avoid exaggerations or omissions. Let your words reflect reality. For example, instead of saying, "I've done everything," specify what actions you've taken and where you could improve.

Admit Mistakes. When you fall short, own up to it. Say, "I made an error, and here's how I'll fix it," rather than shifting blame.

Align Words and Actions. Be consistent in what you say and do. Let your commitments be promises you keep.

Honesty requires courage, but it also creates freedom. When you live transparently, you eliminate the burden of maintaining facades and invite genuine connections.

Weekly Review: The Mirror of Growth

Regular reflection is essential for cultivating accountability and integrity. It provides the space to evaluate your actions, celebrate successes, and identify areas for improvement.

Reflect on Actions. Ask yourself, "Did my actions align with my values? Did I take responsibility where it was needed?"

Identify Growth Opportunities. Highlight moments where you could have acted with greater integrity or accountability.

Celebrate Successes. Recognize instances where you lived authentically, no matter how small. For example, "I kept my promise to deliver on time despite challenges." Your Victory Journal dedicated to these reflections can serve as a powerful tool. Over time, it becomes a record of your growth and a guide for future decisions.

Public Commitment Shared Accountability

Accountability thrives in community. When you share your goals with someone you trust, you invite them to support and challenge you, reinforcing your commitment.

Choose a Trusted Partner. Select someone who will encourage you and hold you accountable without judgment.

Be Specific. Clearly articulate your goals and the steps you'll take to achieve them. Accept feedback and seek counsel from your chosen trusted partner.

Schedule Check-Ins. Meet regularly to discuss progress, challenges, and adjustments. Public commitments transform accountability into a shared journey, fostering mutual growth and support.

Integrity in Leadership: The Power of Example

Integrity is the cornerstone of leadership. Leaders who act with integrity inspire trust and loyalty, creating environments where honesty and accountability thrive.

On my planet, leaders are chosen not for their power but for their wisdom and integrity. Here on Earth, I've observed the desire for the same truth: the most influential leaders are those who lead by example. They hold themselves to the same standards they expect of others, earning the respect and admiration of their teams. These leaders spend their lives building others.

On my planet, integrity is viewed as a cosmic alignment—a harmony between one's actions and the universal principles of truth and justice. Accountability, in turn, is a sacred duty, a commitment to honor the trust placed in us by others.

Here on Earth, I've seen these principles tested by the complexities of modern life. Yet, I've also witnessed extraordinary examples of integrity, from individuals who own their mistakes to communities that come together in pursuit of a common good. These moments reaffirm the transformative power of accountability and integrity, even amidst challenges.

Dear friend, accountability and integrity are not burdens—they are freedoms. They liberate you from the weight of excuses and align your life with your highest values.

Vega's Cosmic Truth: "Accountability is the willingness to own your path. Integrity is the courage to walk it with authenticity."

Embrace these principles as guiding stars on your journey. Live with honesty, take responsibility, and hold yourself to the highest standard of character. In doing so, you will not only elevate your own life but also inspire others to do the same.

Let us walk this path together, step by step, guided by the compass of accountability and integrity.

Journal Prompt
"Reflect on a time when you had to take responsibility for a mistake. What did you learn from the experience, and how did it shape your character?"

Affirmation
"I take ownership of my actions and align my life with my values. My integrity builds trust and inspires growth."

Exercise
Conduct a weekly review of your actions, noting one area where you demonstrated integrity and one where you can improve.

Share a personal goal with a trusted friend or mentor, inviting them to hold you accountable for progress.

Chapter 10: Adaptability and Flexibility – Thriving Amid Change

The 10th Step to Unlimited Human Success…

Embrace change as a natural and necessary part of life, using it as a catalyst for growth and innovation. Stay rooted in your vision but be willing to adjust your methods as circumstances evolve. Trust that even unexpected changes serve a higher purpose, providing opportunities for learning and progress.

Change is the heartbeat of the cosmos. Stars shift, planets realign, and even the most steadfast celestial bodies adapt to the forces around them. On my home planet, adaptability is revered as the ability to flow with life's currents without losing sight of one's purpose. Here on Earth, I've seen this same principle play out in the lives of resilient humans who navigate change with grace and determination.

Your sacred scripture offers wisdom for these moments:

"If any of you lack wisdom, let him ask of God, that giveth to all men liberally, and upbraideth not." (James 1:5)

When faced with uncertainty, seeking wisdom allows you to move forward with confidence and clarity. Adaptability is not about abandoning your goals; it is about finding new paths to achieve them while maintaining faith in your ultimate destination.

Adaptability is the ability to adjust your mindset, strategies, and actions in response to evolving circumstances. It requires flexibility, creativity, and the willingness to embrace the unknown.

Flexibility is not weakness; it is a sign of resilience. It means holding your vision steady while being open to different ways of achieving it.

Faith anchors you in moments of change. It reminds you that challenges are not obstacles but opportunities to grow closer to your divine purpose.

Building Adaptability and Flexibility: Practices and Habits

Embrace Change. A Habit for Growth

Change is inevitable, but your response to it defines your success. By cultivating a mindset that welcomes change, you transform uncertainty into opportunity.

Reframe Your Perspective. Instead of resisting change, view it as an adventure. Ask, "What new possibilities does this bring?"

Practice Acceptance. Understand that change is a natural part of life. By releasing resistance, you free your energy for constructive action.

Stay Curious. Approach change with an open mind, exploring new opportunities and perspectives with enthusiasm.

Example: Imagine a shift in your career path. Instead of focusing on the disruption, consider how it might lead you to discover hidden talents or passions.

Learn New Skills. Expanding Your Toolbox

Continuous learning equips you to adapt to any situation, providing tools to navigate the unexpected.

Identify Growth Areas. Reflect on skills that could enhance your adaptability. For example, learning to communicate effectively in challenging situations.

Start Small. Commit to one new skill at a time. Break it into manageable steps, like dedicating 15 minutes daily to practice.

Leverage Resources. Use online courses, books, or mentors to guide your learning journey.

Practice Consistently. Repetition builds mastery. Dedicate regular time to developing your chosen skill. Example: During a major life change, learning stress-management techniques could help you maintain focus and clarity.

Daily Problem-Solving: A Routine for Innovation

Adaptability thrives when you develop a proactive approach to challenges. Make daily problem-solving a habit to strengthen your resilience.

Identify One Challenge. Each day, choose a specific problem to address, whether big or small.

Brainstorm Solutions. Generate creative approaches without judgment, allowing new ideas to emerge.

Act and Reflect. Implement your chosen solution, then evaluate its effectiveness. Adjust as needed. Example: If a project stalls due to unforeseen issues, brainstorm alternative strategies to move forward, reflecting on lessons learned after each attempt.

Use Faith to Foster Adaptability

Faith is a powerful tool for navigating change. It provides the courage to take steps forward, even when the outcome is uncertain.

Seek Guidance. Begin with prayer or meditation, asking for clarity and wisdom.

Trust the Process. Believe that every change serves a purpose, even if it's not immediately clear.

Take Action in Faith. Move forward with confidence, trusting that the right path will unfold as you act. Example: When faced with a difficult decision, trust that divine guidance will illuminate your way as you take steps toward resolution.

On my planet, we say, *"The wind finds a way around."* This reflects the essence of adaptability—finding new ways forward without losing direction.

Here on Earth, I have seen this principle in action, from individuals overcoming personal hardships to communities innovating in the face of global challenges. These stories reveal a universal truth: adaptability is the key to resilience, and flexibility opens the door to boundless opportunities.

Life's unpredictability is not a barrier; it is an invitation to grow. By embracing adaptability and flexibility, you align yourself with the natural flow of the universe, opening doors to possibilities you may never have imagined.

Vega's Cosmic Truth: "Change is the rhythm of the cosmos. Adaptability is the dance."

As you move forward, let change inspire you to innovate, learn, and thrive. Trust in the divine plan, cultivate a mindset of curiosity and resilience, and step boldly into the unknown. Together, we can transform challenges into stepping stones on the path to unlimited success.

Journal Prompt:
"Reflect on a time when unexpected change led to personal growth. What did you learn, and how did it shape your perspective?"

Affirmation:

"I welcome change as an opportunity to grow. With faith and adaptability, I can thrive in any circumstance."

Exercise:

Identify one area of your life where you've been resisting change. Write down three ways to reframe it as an opportunity for growth.

Practice brainstorming solutions to a current challenge using the steps outlined in daily problem-solving.

Chapter 11: Faith in God's Timing – Trusting the Eternal Clockwork

The 11th Step to Unlimited Human Success…

The Creator's timeline is vast, intricate, and beyond human comprehension, ensuring the greatest good rather than the quickest result. Waiting is not wasted time; it is a sacred period of growth, preparation, and alignment with divine will. Persistence in your efforts complements patience in divine timing, creating a balance that propels you forward in harmony with God's plan.

Timing is both a mystery and a miracle. On my planet, we measure time in the flow of celestial rivers and the cycles of stars—movements so precise that even the smallest deviation could disrupt the balance of our universe. Earth's approach to time is different: human lives are woven with an urgency born from your mortality, a need to measure moments and achieve swiftly. Yet, as I've observed, the most profound breakthroughs often emerge not in haste, but in the stillness of trust.

Your sacred scripture declares:

"And let us not be weary in well doing: for in due season we shall reap, if we faint not." (Gal. 6:9)

This verse holds a universal truth: the foundation of greatness is built not only through action but through faith in the timing of that action's fruition.

When I first crash-landed in Las Vegas, my desperation to get home mirrored humanity's tendency to force solutions when answers seem delayed. I scoured your city for resources, meeting resistance at every turn. Frustration consumed me until a quiet moment with a homeless man named David shifted my perspective.

"You can't rush what's meant to be," David said. "Sometimes the waiting is the work." His words, simple yet profound, felt like a whisper from the cosmos. I began to see my delays not as obstacles but as opportunities. The waiting became a teacher, urging me to grow, reflect, and prepare for what lay ahead. My earthly detour became a divine journey, shaped by our Creator's perfect timing.

Faith in God's timing is not passive resignation—it is an active surrender, a choice to align your will with divine wisdom. Humans often measure success by speed, but the Creator's clock operates on a higher plane, orchestrating events to bring about the greatest blessings in their due season.

Just as a farmer does not demand an immediate harvest but nurtures the soil, plants the seeds, and trusts the sun and rain, so too must you trust the process of growth and fruition in your life.

Building Faith in God's Timing: Practices and Habits

Trust in God's Plan

Developing trust begins with the recognition that God's wisdom surpasses human understanding.

Reaffirm Your Faith. Reflect on past experiences where waiting led to unexpected blessings. Write these moments down to remind yourself of God's hand in your life.

Release Control. Let go of the need to dictate outcomes. Use affirmations like, "I trust in

God's perfect timing," or "The Creator's plan unfolds in divine order."

Celebrate Progress. Focus on small steps, recognizing that each one brings you closer to your ultimate goal. Example: If a long-awaited opportunity remains elusive, shift your focus to the skills, relationships, or insights you're gaining in the on the way to that experience.

Seek Divine Guidance

Prayer and reflection transform waiting from passive endurance to active participation in the Creator's plan.

How to Seek Guidance:

Pray with Purpose. In your prayers, ask for patience, clarity, and strength to trust the timing of God's answers. Example: "Grant me the wisdom to wait with faith and the courage to act when the time is right."

Reflect Daily. Spend time journaling about lessons you're learning during periods of waiting. What growth is this season inviting?

Immerse Yourself in Inspiration. Read scriptures, sacred texts, or stories that highlight the power of divine timing. Let these serve as reminders of God's faithfulness. Surround yourself with music, people, and entertainment that uplifts and inspires you.

Wait with Intention

Waiting is not idle—it is a period of preparation, growth, and alignment.

Embrace the Pause. Use moments of waiting to recharge and prepare. Instead of filling every moment with activity, take time to rest, meditate, or learn.

Observe God's Signs. Pay attention to subtle guidance—an unexpected opportunity, a chance meeting, or a sudden insight.

Persist in Effort. Continue working toward your goals with patience, knowing that the Creator's timing will align with your efforts. A delayed promotion at work could be an opportunity to strengthen your skills, deepen relationships, or explore new interests.

On my planet, the concept of the "Eternal Flow" mirrors your understanding of divine timing. Every delay, every challenge, every moment of waiting serves a purpose in the grand design of existence.

Across Earth's spiritual traditions, I've found stories that echo this truth: Joseph's rise to leadership in Egypt, the patience of Job, the endurance of the early pioneers of faith. These examples reveal that waiting is not wasted—it is sacred.

I invite you to embrace the sacred rhythm of God's timing. Trust that every delay is a lesson, every unanswered prayer is an invitation to grow, and every moment of waiting is a step closer to the fulfillment of your divine potential.

Vega's Cosmic Truth: "The Creator's clock runs not on haste but on harmony, aligning every moment with the greater good."

Take heart, for you are laying the foundation of a great work. Move forward with patience, faith, and trust in the eternal clockwork. Together, we'll navigate the divine timing of the cosmos, unlocking the infinite potential within and around us.

Journal Prompt:
"Reflect on a time when waiting led to an unexpected blessing. What lessons did you learn, and how did your faith grow during that season?"

Affirmation:

"I trust in the Creator's perfect timing. Each moment of waiting prepares me for the blessings to come."

Exercise:

Write a letter to your future self, describing your hopes and faith in God's plan. Revisit this letter during challenging times to remind yourself of your trust in divine timing.

Chapter 12: Learning and Personal Growth – A Journey Beyond the Stars

The 12th Step to Unlimited Human Success...

Intelligence and truth are eternal. Every lesson learned in this life becomes part of your eternal soul, preparing you for growth beyond mortality. Learning is not merely the accumulation of facts but the application of truth to refine character and inspire action. Your mortal life is a sacred curriculum designed to refine you through lessons in love, resilience, service, and faith.

In the expanse of the cosmos, learning is the foundation of all progress and creation. On my home planet, the pursuit of knowledge is our greatest joy, a journey without end. Each insight gained is seen as a thread in the infinite tapestry of existence, connecting us to the Creator and to one another.

Here on Earth, I've marveled at humanity's thirst for understanding. Your ability to not only seek knowledge but also transform it into wisdom is a reflection of your divine heritage. As your scripture beautifully states:

"But to be learned is good if they hearken unto the counsels of God." (2 Nephi 9:29)

This truth is universal: learning is sacred when it is anchored in purpose and aligned with eternal principles.

Earth is not simply a destination—it is a classroom, and every lesson you embrace here prepares you for your eternal journey. The intelligence you gain, the skills you develop, and the truths you uncover are not lost when this mortal life ends. They become eternal possessions, tools for creation and service in the life to come.

Think of learning as planting seeds in a garden that you will tend forever. Each piece of knowledge, each act of growth, is a seed that will flourish into greater understanding, wisdom, and joy in the eternities.

Building a Lifelong Habit of Learning

Daily Reading. Feeding the Mind and Spirit Through reading, you unlock the wisdom of ages, the insights of diverse cultures, and the teachings of inspired minds.

Set Aside Sacred Time. Dedicate a specific part of your day—whether morning, midday, or evening—to reading. Consistency is key to growth. Balance Your Knowledge Diet: Include spiritual texts, uplifting literature, and practical knowledge to enrich both your intellect and spirit. For example:

Spiritual Growth: Study scripture or other inspired writings that deepen your understanding of divine truths.

Personal Development: Read books that challenge your perspective and inspire action.
Practical Skills: Explore topics that enhance your ability to serve and succeed.

Engage with the Material. Don't just read passively; reflect on the lessons. Ask, "What does this mean for me? How can I use this knowledge to grow?"

Ask Questions and Seek Answers

Curiosity is the spark that ignites growth. Every great discovery begins with a question, and every meaningful answer inspires further inquiry. How to Cultivate Curiosity:

Be a Lifelong Student. View every experience as an opportunity to learn. When faced with challenges, ask, "What is this teaching me?"

Seek Mentors. Surround yourself with individuals who inspire and challenge you. Learn from their wisdom, mistakes, and successes.

Engage in Dialogue. Share your questions and insights with others. Collaboration often leads to breakthroughs that solitary effort cannot achieve. Example: If you're curious about a skill, seek out an expert who can guide you, or explore online courses and communities dedicated to the topic.

Reflect and Apply: Turning Knowledge into Wisdom

Learning without application is like gathering seeds but never planting them. The power of knowledge lies in its ability to transform your actions, relationships, and purpose.

End Each Day with Reflection. Ask yourself, "What did I learn today? How has this changed my understanding?"

Keep a Growth Journal. Document your insights and lessons. Over time, this journal becomes a record of your progress and a source of inspiration.

Experiment Boldly. Apply what you've learned in real-life situations. Be willing to make mistakes—they are part of the learning process. Example: If you read about leadership, practice applying one principle in your interactions the next day. Reflect on what worked and what didn't, and refine your approach.

Earth is a sacred school designed by the Creator to refine and prepare you for your divine potential. Its lessons extend beyond academics, encompassing experiences in love, resilience, service, and faith. Every interaction, trial, and triumph offers an opportunity to grow closer to your divine purpose.

On my planet, we say, "Truth is the currency of eternity." Each truth you gain here increases your capacity for joy and creation in the life to come. By embracing learning as a lifelong journey, you prepare yourself for the infinite possibilities that await.

The pursuit of knowledge is eternal, and Earth is your sacred classroom. Embrace the challenges, questions, and opportunities that come your way as divine invitations to grow. Every truth you uncover, every skill you master, and every lesson you apply becomes part of the infinite potential within you.

Together, let us embark on this journey of growth and discovery. Your spirit is boundless, and the lessons you learn today will echo into eternity. Seek, serve, and become more than you ever imagined—your destiny as a divine creator awaits.

———

Journal Prompt:
"What is one lesson I've learned this week, and how has it shaped my understanding or actions? How can I apply this lesson tomorrow?"

Affirmation:
"I am a lifelong learner, embracing each moment as an opportunity to grow, serve, and discover truth."

Exercise:
Create a *Learning Plan* for the next month. Identify one skill, topic, or principle you want to master. Break it into weekly goals and document your progress.

Chapter 13: Service and Generosity – The Heart of True Success

The 13th Step to Unlimited Human Success...

True service transcends self-interest, reflecting the divine nature of humanity and fostering profound connections. Giving selflessly enriches both the giver and the receiver, creating ripples of goodness that extend far beyond the initial act. A life of service and generosity aligns with the Creator's purpose, offering fulfillment that transcends material gains.

Service and generosity are not merely acts of kindness; they are expressions of divine love. On my planet, service is considered the highest form of respect for others, and generosity is a sacred duty. Earth's sacred texts echo this truth. One verse that profoundly resonates is:

"Give, and it shall be given unto you; good measure, pressed down, and shaken together, and running over,

shall men give into your bosom. For with the same measure that ye mete withal it shall be measured to you again." (Luke 6:38)

This principle is universal, as you serve and give, you align yourself with the Creator's purpose, inviting blessings that enrich your life in ways beyond measure.

During the last couple years of my time on Earth, I've witnessed the transformative power of service. One memory that stands out involves Alvin, a janitor with a heart full of generosity. Despite his modest income, he brought breakfast every morning to a homeless man outside his workplace. When I asked why, Alvin simply said, "Because it's what I can do. And when I do it, I feel rich."

Alvin's story illustrates a profound truth: the joy of service lies not in its scale but in its sincerity. Acts of service, no matter how small, uplift both the giver and the receiver, creating a wealth of spirit that transcends material possessions.

Building a Life of Service and Generosity

Every day presents opportunities to serve others, and even the simplest gestures can create meaningful connections.

Start Your Day with Intention. Each morning, ask yourself, "Who can I serve today?" Whether it's offering a kind word, assisting a colleague, or lending a hand to a neighbor, small acts of kindness build a life of service.

Be Present in Your Sphere. Look for ways to serve those closest to you—family, friends, or colleagues. Often, the greatest opportunities are right before you.

Celebrate the Impact. Reflect on your acts of service at the end of each day. Acknowledge how they brought joy or relief to others and enriched your own spirit.

Generosity Through Tithing and Charity

Generosity extends beyond time and effort to include your resources. Tithing and charitable giving are powerful ways to express gratitude and contribute to the greater good.

Practice Tithing. Give a portion of your income as an act of faith and gratitude. As promised in scripture:

"Bring ye all the tithes into the storehouse... and prove me now herewith, saith the Lord of hosts, if I will not open you the windows of heaven, and pour you out a blessing, that there shall not be room enough to receive it." (Malachi 3:10)

We have similar promises from God on my planet. I have personally tested this principle and in difficult moments, when I did not have enough resources for myself, I chose to give and was rewarded greatly. You will be too.

Support Meaningful Causes. Identify charitable organizations or initiatives that resonate with your values. Whether funding education, supporting food banks, or donating to medical research, your contributions can create lasting change.

Remember the Widow's Mite. Generosity is not measured by the amount but by the love and sacrifice behind it. Even small gifts, given with sincerity, carry immense power.

Volunteer Work: Service on a Larger Scale

Volunteering allows you to extend your impact and create lasting change within your community.

Choose a Cause That Inspires You. Reflect on your passions and identify a cause that aligns with them—mentoring youth, environmental conservation, or supporting healthcare initiatives.

Commit to Consistency. Dedicate time regularly, whether monthly or weekly, to volunteer. Consistency transforms service into a way of life.

Involve Others. Invite family or friends to join your efforts. Shared service strengthens relationships and amplifies the impact of your generosity.

Service as the True Measure of Success

Generosity creates ripples that extend far beyond the initial act. When you give selflessly, you inspire others to do the same, fostering a culture of kindness and connection. As scripture reminds us:

"He which soweth sparingly shall reap also sparingly; and he which soweth bountifully shall reap also bountifully." (2 Corinthians 9:6)

I've witnessed this principle firsthand. A single act of generosity can ignite a chain reaction, inspiring others to pay it forward and multiplying the goodness in the world.

True success is not about accumulation but contribution. It is measured by the lives you touch, the burdens you ease, and the joy you spread. Service and generosity connect you to the divine, reminding you that your purpose is to uplift and inspire others.

When you serve selflessly and give generously, you align your actions with eternal principles, building a legacy that transcends your mortal life.

Embrace service and generosity as guiding principles in your life. Look for opportunities to uplift others daily, share your resources with gratitude, and commit to causes that inspire you.

The joy of giving is limitless. The more you serve, the richer your spirit becomes. Together, let us create a world where love and generosity flow freely, lifting humanity to its highest potential.

Let's sow seeds of kindness, knowing they will bear fruit for generations to come. In service and generosity, you will find the heart of true success.

Journal Prompt:

"What is one act of service or generosity I can commit to this week? How can I use my time, talents, or resources to uplift someone else?"

Affirmation:

"I find joy and purpose in serving others. My generosity creates ripples of goodness that extend beyond my sight."

Exercise:

Gratitude and Service Plan: At the start of each week, identify one person you can serve and one cause to which you can contribute. Reflect on these efforts at week's end to recognize their impact.

Chapter 14: Hope and Optimism – A Light in the Darkness

The 14th Step to Unlimited Human Success...

Hope is a guiding light, a deliberate choice that connects you to divine potential and resilience. Optimism transforms hope into movement, empowering you to face challenges and pursue opportunities. Positive self-talk, gratitude, and visualization anchor your mindset in positivity and progress.

Hope is not merely a flicker of wishful thinking—it is a powerful force that sustains the human spirit through life's darkest moments. Optimism, its close companion, is hope in action, guiding you to see possibilities where others see limitations.

As your earth scripture teaches:

"Now the God of hope fill you with all joy and peace in believing, that ye may abound in hope, through the power of the Holy Ghost." (Romans 15:13)

This verse encapsulates the transformative potential of hope. It is a divine gift that brings joy and peace, enabling you to navigate uncertainty with faith and perseverance.

When I arrived here. my immediate focus was survival, and the challenges of adapting to this unfamiliar world felt insurmountable. It was the unwavering hope I observed in humans that inspired me to see beyond my circumstances.

Elias, a man I met in Las Vegas, embodied this principle. Despite losing his home and livelihood, he told me, *"As long as the sun rises, there's a chance for things to get better."* His resilience showed me that hope is not a naïve dream but a conscious decision to trust in the possibility of brighter days.

Through Elias, I learned that hope is the refusal to let despair dictate your actions. It is the courage to believe in new possibilities, even when the path forward is unclear.

Optimism is the proactive counterpart to hope—it sees challenges as stepping stones and embraces setbacks as lessons. Maria, a young artist

I met, personified optimism. After years of rejection, she persisted, saying, *"Every 'no' brings me closer to the 'yes' I'm waiting for."*

Her mindset fueled her perseverance, and eventually, her work found its audience. Optimism, like hope, is not blind to difficulties. Instead, it focuses on the opportunities within those difficulties, transforming obstacles into catalysts for growth.

Habits to Cultivate Hope and Optimism

Positive Self-Talk. Rewiring Your Mindset: Your internal dialogue shapes your reality. Practicing positive self-talk reinforces hope and optimism, even in challenging times.

    Morning Affirmations. Begin your day with affirmations such as:

"I trust that good things are coming my way."

"I am capable of overcoming any challenge."

"The future is filled with endless possibilities."

Reframe Negativity. Replace limiting thoughts like *"I can't do this"* with empowering ones like *"I haven't figured this out yet, but I will."*

Create a Positive Environment. Surround yourself with uplifting quotes, music, and messages that inspire hope.

Gratitude: Finding Light in Challenges

Gratitude shifts your focus from scarcity to abundance, cultivating a mindset that nurtures hope.

Daily Gratitude Journal. Each evening, write down three things you're grateful for, no matter how small. A kind smile, a warm meal, or a moment of laughter are all worthy of recognition.

Reframe Struggles. During challenges, ask yourself, *"What lesson can I learn from this? What small blessing can I find in this experience?"*

Express Gratitude to Others. Share your appreciation with those around you, strengthening connections and fostering positivity.

Visualization: Seeing the Future You Desire

Visualization aligns your thoughts and actions with your goals, creating a mental blueprint for success.

Create a Clear Vision. Spend time each day visualizing your goals as if they've already been achieved. Imagine the sights, sounds, and emotions of your success.

Feel the Emotions. Allow yourself to experience the joy, pride, and fulfillment of realizing your dreams.

Combine with Prayer. After visualizing, offer a prayer of gratitude and seek guidance in taking the necessary steps forward.

Hope as a Spiritual Principle

Hope is a divine gift, a reminder that you are not alone in your journey. As scripture assures:

"For I know the thoughts that I think toward you, saith the Lord, thoughts of peace, and not of evil, to give you an expected end." (Jeremiah 29:11)

This promise underscores the Creator's plan for your life—one filled with purpose, growth, and joy. Trusting in this plan allows you to face uncertainty with confidence, knowing you are guided by divine wisdom.

On my home planet, hope is seen as the thread that connects all beings to their divine potential. It is the belief that even in the vastness of the cosmos, each life has meaning and purpose. Here on Earth, I've witnessed hope bridge the gap between despair and possibility, uniting individuals in their shared journey toward growth. Hope is not passive—it is the foundation of resilience, creativity, and transformation. It is the ember that sparks change, illuminating the path forward even in the darkest times.

Please make hope and optimism your daily companions. Choose to believe in a brighter future and act with faith and determination. Cultivate habits of positive self-talk, gratitude, and visualization to anchor your mindset in resilience and possibility.

Hope is not a fleeting emotion—it is a powerful force that aligns you with divine purpose and opens the door to infinite potential. Together, let us illuminate the world with the light of hope, building a future filled with joy, growth, and boundless opportunities.

The future is vast, waiting for you to shape it. Choose hope today, and let it guide you toward the life you are destined to create.

—

Journal Prompt:

"What is one challenge I'm currently facing, and how can I find hope and opportunity within it?"

Affirmation:

"I choose hope and optimism as my guiding lights. I trust in the divine plan and my ability to create a brighter future."

Exercise:

Create a Vision Board: Gather images, quotes, and symbols that represent your goals and dreams. Place it somewhere you'll see daily, using it as a visual reminder of your hope-filled future.

Chapter 15: Prayer and Connection with God

The 11th Step to Unlimited Human Success...

Prayer is more than speaking—it's a dialogue that fosters a personal connection with God. Consistent, intentional prayer transforms your daily life into a sacred journey. Focus, persistence, and trust help you maintain a meaningful prayer life even in difficult moments.

Prayer is the language of the soul, a sacred dialogue between you and the Creator. It is an act of humility, trust, and faith that aligns your heart with divine wisdom. Your scriptures beautifully illustrate this principle:

"Therefore may God grant unto you, my brethren, that ye may begin to exercise your faith unto repentance, that ye begin to call upon his holy name, that he would have mercy upon you;

Yea, cry unto him for mercy; for he is mighty to save. Yea, humble yourselves, and continue in prayer unto him. Cry unto him in your houses, yea, over all your household, both morning, mid-day, and evening.

Yea, cry unto him against the power of your enemies. Yea, cry unto him against the devil, who is an enemy to all righteousness.

Cry unto him over the crops off your fields, that ye may prosper in them. Cry over the flocks of your fields, that they may increase.

But this is not all; ye must pour out your souls in your closets, and your secret places, and in your wilderness. Yea, and when you do not cry unto the Lord, let your hearts be full, drawn out in prayer unto him continually for your welfare, and also for the welfare of those who are around you." (Alma 34:17-27)

Prayer is not merely a ritual—it is a relationship. Through prayer, you invite divine guidance, express gratitude, and seek alignment with God's will. It transforms your life, bringing clarity, strength, and peace amid uncertainty. It secures blessings that God wants to give you, blessings that are unlocked by asking and seeking.

When I first began to pray under the neon glow of Las Vegas, I questioned whether the Creator of the cosmos would hear the pleas of a stranded traveler from another world. But as I knelt and offered my heart, I felt a profound stillness, a quiet assurance that transcended words. Prayer is a lifeline, connecting us to the Creator's infinite wisdom and love.

Prayer matters because it is transformative. It helps you align your desires with God's will, strengthens your faith, and provides comfort in times of trial. It is through prayer that you find clarity in confusion, strength in weakness, and light in darkness.

Building a Life of Prayer: Practices and Habits

Daily Prayer: A Lifelong Dialogue. Daily prayer is the foundation of your spiritual journey. By beginning and ending your day with prayer, you create a rhythm that centers your life around God's guidance.

Morning Prayer. Begin each day with gratitude and seek guidance for the challenges ahead. Pray for strength, wisdom, and opportunities to serve.

Evening Prayer. Reflect on your day, express gratitude for your blessings, and seek forgiveness for any missteps. Ask for peace and rest as you prepare for a new day.

Write Your Prayers. If you struggle with focus, write your prayers in your journal. This practice clarifies your thoughts and creates a tangible record of your spiritual growth.

Morning and Evening Devotions: A Sacred Routine

Devotion deepens your connection with God by combining prayer, scripture study, and reflection.

Incorporate Scripture. Read from sacred texts that inspire and challenge you. Reflect on their application in your life.

Create a Quiet Space. Set aside a peaceful area where you can connect with God without distractions.

Reflect and Listen. After reading or praying, spend a few moments in silence. Trust that divine impressions will come in their time.

Family Prayer: Strengthening Relationships

Prayer is not only a personal practice but a communal one. Family prayer brings unity, love, and shared purpose to your household.

Set a Regular Time. Choose a consistent time, such as after dinner or before bed, for family prayer.

Encourage Participation. Invite each family member to share their thoughts, gratitude, or concerns.

Focus on Togetherness. Use family prayer as a time to pray for one another and seek God's guidance as a unit.

Overcoming Challenges in Prayer

Prayer, though simple, is not always easy. Distractions, doubts, and discouragement can create obstacles. Here's how to navigate them:

When You Feel Distant from God. Approach prayer with humility and persistence, trusting that God hears you even when His presence feels distant.

When You Struggle to Focus. Create a quiet environment, write down your prayer, or continue to bring your thoughts back to communication with God.

When You're Discouraged. Share your struggles openly with God. Remember that trials often precede growth, and answers come in His time.

On my home planet, prayer is seen as a form of spiritual resonance, aligning the soul with the Creator's light. It is not just a means of asking but a way of becoming, transforming desires into divine action.

Here on Earth, I've seen prayer transcend cultures, languages, and circumstances. It is a universal connection that unites all beings with their Creator, providing guidance, strength, and peace.

Prayer is work, but it is the most rewarding work you will ever undertake. It transforms ordinary moments into sacred experiences, aligning your will with God's and unveiling your divine potential.

As you commit to a life of prayer, you will see God's hand in your journey. Prayer becomes a source of strength, a wellspring of peace, and a beacon of hope.

I invite you to make prayer an integral part of your life. Begin today, whether with a simple word of thanks or a heartfelt plea for guidance. Commit to daily prayer, devotions, and family prayer. Let prayer become the thread that weaves your life into God's divine plan.

Prayer is not just about asking—it is about connecting, listening, and aligning. It is the key to unlocking your potential and living a life of peace, purpose, and joy.

Together, let us draw closer to the Creator, who knows us, loves us, and desires our ultimate success. Let prayer guide your journey, illuminate your path, and reveal the divine potential within you.

Journal Prompt:
"What blessings have I received recently, and how can I express gratitude to God in my prayers?"

Affirmation:
"I trust in God's wisdom and seek His guidance through daily prayer. My heart is open, my spirit aligned, and my faith strengthened."

Exercise:
Create a Prayer Space: Dedicate a small area in your home for prayer and reflection. Include items that inspire reverence, such as scriptures, meaningful symbols, or a gratitude jar.

Conclusion: Becoming the Architect of Your Unlimited Success

As we reach the conclusion of this journey, I invite you to pause and reflect on how far you've come—not just through the pages of this book but in the life you've built thus far. You have in your mind all of the steps that will lead you to unlimited success. You have explored universal truths, embraced eternal principles, and begun unlocking the divine potential within you. You have the tools, the knowledge, and the faith to manifest the life you've always dreamed of. But let me remind you of a vital truth: this is not the end. It is only the beginning.

When we began, I promised you that applying the principles in this book would make your dreams achievable, your goals clearer, and your potential limitless. Let's revisit those promises and see how they've come to life:

Your Dreams Are Now Within Reach Through vision and goal-setting, discipline, and faith, you've transformed your hopes into tangible actions. You've learned to clarify your desires, break them into achievable steps, and trust in the divine timing that guides all things.

You Are Stronger Than Ever Before By cultivating habits of persistence, adaptability, and resilience, you've discovered an unshakable strength within yourself. Challenges that once seemed insurmountable now serve as stepping stones toward your success.

You Are Connected to the Infinite Prayer, gratitude, and service have deepened your connection to the Creator, to others, and to your highest self. You now see that life is not about accumulating achievements but about aligning with eternal truths and living a life of meaning and love.

You Are Equipped to Transform Your Life With practical tools like time management, emotional intelligence, and optimism, you've built a foundation for lasting success. You've learned that success is not just about what you do but about who you become.

The principles you've learned are timeless, but their power lies in your willingness to apply them consistently. As you move forward, remember these guiding truths:

You Are Divine. Your potential is infinite because you were created by a divine hand. Never doubt your worth or capacity to achieve greatness. Faith and Action Go Hand in Hand: Trust in God's plan, but also take bold steps toward your goals. Faith without action is a wish; faith with action is a miracle waiting to happen.

Service and Love Are the True Measures of Success. The more you give, the more you receive—not just in material wealth but in joy, purpose, and connection.

You Are Never Alone. The Creator walks with you, guiding and supporting you through every challenge and triumph.

Dear reader, the cosmos is vast, but your purpose shines brighter than any star. You have everything you need to become the architect of your success, to build a life of abundance, joy, and meaning.

The principles in this book are not merely ideas—they are the keys to unlocking your divine potential. Apply them with faith, persistence, and love, and you will not only achieve your goals but also inspire others to do the same.

The universe is waiting for your light. Rise boldly, live authentically, and let your brilliance illuminate the world.

With cosmic admiration and unwavering belief in your potential,

Vega Sparx

Your Eternal Guide to Unlimited Human Success

www.ingramcontent.com/pod-product-compliance
Lightning Source LLC
Chambersburg PA
CBHW061801070526
44586CB00023B/2665